Extract from Treasure Island

Year 3 activities

Word level

Explore unusual vocabulary.

Compare words showing movement: *plodding, stroll, leap, run, pursue.* Build other words based on them: *plod, plodded,* etc.

Sentence level

Point out the conventions of setting out speech: speech marks, and new paragraph when speech begins.

Identify the verbs in the extract and discuss their meaning and function.

Text level

Illustrate the strength of the character of Billy Bones through effective reading.

Ask the class what facts they learn about the narrator of the story.

Point out that this passage comes from the opening of a story called *Treasure Island.*

What might the whole story be about?
What part might these characters play in such a story?
Why might Billy Bones be so afraid of the one-legged sailor?

Talk about the effect all this has on Jim, as shown in the last paragraph.

Group work and individual writing

Work on the scene where Billy Bones asks Jim to keep a look-out. Write this in direct speech.

Write and illustrate a police 'Wanted Poster' for Billy Bones.

Make up a list of items that Billy Bones might have in his chest. Does the title of the book give any clues?

Work on a performance of the arrival of Billy Bones at the Admiral Benbow. This could be rewritten in play form.

Find and read poems by Robert Louis Stevenson such as *From a Railway Carriage,* or *Windy Nights.*

Year 4 activities

Word level

Find alternative words for:
tall, strong, heavy, nut-brown, ragged, scarred, dirty, livid.

Sentence level

Pick out and discuss the strong verbs used in the last paragraph.

Look at the use of the adverbs: *roughly, coarsely.*

Look at the sentence beginning 'And, indeed'. Rework into two sentences in a more modern style, making the meaning clearer.

Practise reading aloud some of the longer sentences, using punctuation correctly to show sentence structure and emphasis.

Text level

Talk about how the individual details of the description of Billy Bones help to build up a picture of him.

Talk about how the author uses the description of the weather in the last paragraph to emphasise

Jim's nightmare feelings and make the paragraph more horrifying.

Look closely at the description of Billy Bones' voice, and how Stevenson uses figurative language to describe it.

Look at the way the passage is divided into paragraphs, and the subject of each.

Group work and individual writing

Write character sketches of Billy Bones based on the extract.

Write an imaginative playscript involving Billy Bones and the one-legged sailor.

Improvise a 'chat-show' interview for Billy Bones in which he talks about his life at sea.

Ask pupils to imagine that one day Billy Bones receives a letter from the one-legged sailor. What would the letter contain?

Write an extract from Jim's diary.

LITERACY LINE-UP
TEACHER'S BOOK

CONTENTS

INTRODUCTION

These notes link the texts in the three Literacy Line-up pupil books to the content of the National Literacy Strategy framework for teaching for Key Stage 2. The notes are not exhaustive, and are intended to support the teacher's own planning rather than be a complete scheme of work in themselves. Revising and revisiting work is an important element of the framework, so teachers working with Year 4, 5 and 6 pupils should also bear in mind relevant work from previous years when using these notes.

Most teachers will use the requirement on the range of texts to be studied as a starting point for their planning. For example, the Year 3, term 2 range mentions 'myths, legends, fables, parables'. King Midas is clearly an appropriate text to address that requirement, but it would be a pity to limit it to that term, as the word level and sentence level content may well be useful at other times – showing how words and phrases signal time sequences, for example (Year 3 term 3).

Some texts are more challenging than others but it is hoped that the ideas in these notes will allow teachers to make use of these texts right through the key stage.

Year 5 activities

Word Level

Look at the meanings of the 'horror' words in the last paragraph:
haunted, diabolical, monstrous, nightmare, abominable.
Use dictionaries to explore their meanings and derivation.

Look at the figure of speech 'keep a weather eye open', and learn its meaning.

Compare the words *custom* and *accustomed* and discuss meaning. Can any other words be formed from this root?

Sentence level

Look closely at a sentence such as 'Every day, when he came back . . .' and see how its sense would change if the order of the phrases were changed.

Look at the difference between direct and reported speech in the conversation between Billy Bones and Jim's father, and look at how direct speech is set out.

See how although the passage is written in the past tense, occasionally the present tense is used to make the passage come to life in such phrases as 'says he'.

Look at clauses in extended sentences.

Text level

Look at the different ways the character of Billy Bones is presented – through description, speech and action.

Work on an 'author profile' of Stevenson, looking at *Treasure Island* as a whole and other examples of his work including *Kidnapped* and *A Child's Garden of Verses*.

Discuss how effective the extract is as the opening of a novel, and how the author makes the reader want to read on.

The printed extract omits the first paragraph of *Treasure Island*, printed below. Read this to the class, and discuss what further information they have learnt about the story, and how effective this paragraph is in encouraging readers to read on.

> 'Squire Trelawney, Dr Livesey, and the rest of these gentlemen having asked me to write down the whole particulars about Treasure Island, from the beginning to the end, keeping nothing back but the bearings of the island, and that only because there is still treasure not yet lifted, I take up my pen in the year of grace 17 --, and go back to the time when my father kept the 'Admiral Benbow' inn, and the brown old seaman, with the sabre cut, first took lodging under our roof.'

Group work and individual writing

Work on an improvised interview in which Jim as an adult is asked questions about his experiences as a child.

Rewrite the paragraph beginning 'Every day, when he came back . . .' in the third person, using 'Jim' instead of 'I'.

Write an author profile of Stevenson.

Write out the extract in note form using bullet points, e.g.

- Billy Bones arrives at the Admiral Benbow

- He orders a glass of rum

- He decides to stay at the inn.

Write the extract from the point of view of Billy Bones.

Compile a list of questions that the group would like answered about
a the passage

and

b the whole novel.

Year 6 activities

Word level

Explore words in the passage that seem old-fashioned, and find modern equivalents.

Use dictionaries to find the derivation of some of the more unusual vocabulary.

Look at the use of dialect orthography in words such as 'sittyated' and 'moight'.

Find examples of nautical expressions used by Billy Bones.

Sentence level

Look closely at the complex structure of the first sentence in the extract, and how the semi-colon and other punctuation is used.

Identify main and sub-clauses in a selected sentence.

Text level

Explore the chronology of the extract, i.e. When was it written? In what historical period is it set? How old might the narrator be

a at the time of the events described

and

b at the time he wrote them?

Look at the structure of each paragraph and summarise its content.

Group work and individual writing

In the last paragraph of *Treasure Island* Jim says 'Oxen and wain-ropes would not bring me back again to that accursed island.'
Ask groups to discuss what this might tell them about the story of the book as a whole.

Write a back cover blurb for *Treasure Island* based on the group's knowledge and the predictions they have made.

Write a short piece of prose entitled 'The unwelcome visitor' based on the 'flashback' technique, perhaps starting 'I remember him (her) as if it were yesterday.'

A GHOST STORY

Year 3 activities

Word level

Build up unusual words such as *philosopher, Athenodorus,* using phonemes.

Talk about the construction of *ing* words with a dropped e – *write, writing.*

Discuss the meaning of words such as *unkempt, straggly, philosopher, beckoning, excavated, bound.*

Build words based on angry:
anger, angrier, angriest, angered.

Take about the prefix *dis* in disappeared.
Discuss the possible meaning of 'kempt' (formed from *unkempt*).

Sentence level

Look for alternative verbs to *liked, found, shook,* to make the passage more interesting and colourful.

Talk about the use of the past tense in *sat, heard, looked.* Try this in the present tense – how has it changed?

Collect adjectives – *filthy, unkempt, straggly.*
Find others, perhaps using a thesaurus, that could be used to describe the ghost.

Think of adjectives to qualify *house, chains, finger, skeleton.*

Discuss word order and the difference between sentences, such as *a small pile of leaves* and *a pile of small leaves.*

Look at spelling of plurals such as *city – cities.*

Talk about the use of the pronouns *he* and *his.* What if the philosopher or the ghost were female?

Talk about agreement in 'there were chains' and 'there was a house'.

Text level

Talk about other possible story openings:
once, a long time ago, etc.

Talk about how the author could have made the telling of the story more exciting.

Group work and individual writing

Use speech marks in a new section of the story in which an estate agent tries to persuade the philosopher to buy the house, or in which a neighbour tries to persuade him not to buy it!

Design and write a 'For Sale' advertisement for the house.

Present the events of the story as a storyboard.

Year 4 activities

Word level

Talk about double consonants in *straggly, puzzled, followed, disappeared.*

Build words using the prefix *un*: *unmarked, unexcavated, unbound, undressed.*

Talk about plurals for words ending in f: *leaf, leaves.*

Sentence level

Identify adverbs – *suddenly, angrily*.
Discuss suitable adverbs for
'he sat . . . writing at his desk'.

Pick out words showing a time sequence:
was, eventually, about this time, on, then, at first, at last, next.

Discuss comparative and superlative:
loud, louder, loudest.

Rearrange the sentence 'About this time . . . city'
in as many ways as possible.

Join the first two sentences using a conjunction.
Join the sentence beginning 'Next morning' with
the following one.

Text level

Find words to characterise the philosopher.
Why wasn't he afraid?

Identify the structure of the story:
introduction, build-up, climax, resolution.

Discuss how the author builds up the tension in
the story.

Group work and individual writing

Use reference books to find out about Pliny the
Younger, and perhaps read part of his letter
describing the eruption of Vesuvius.

Imagine a previous owner of the house.
Write his or her account of the ghost as a diary
entry, or a letter.

Prepare and perform an interview with the
philosopher for Athens TV.

Year 5 activities

Relevant work from previous years plus:

Word level

Discuss synonyms and phrases for low price – *cheap*, *inexpensive*, *dirt cheap*, *a bargain*, etc.

Find opposites for the words and phrases.

Do the same activity for *interested*. Talk about the difference between *uninterested* and *disinterested*.

Talk about the suffix *ful* in peaceful. Collect other words using this suffix.

Sentence level

List difficult words and find alternatives for a younger audience.

Talk about how commas are used in the third sentence.

Rewrite a sentence in the first person from the point of view of the philosopher.

Find and discuss clauses beginning *at last, then,* and the use of clauses embedded with commas in the first paragraph.

Text level

Discuss possible similes and metaphors that could be used to enhance the description of the ghost and the incidents of the story.

Encourage the class to speculate about the possible reasons for the ghost's behaviour.

Group work and individual writing

Find out more about Pliny and the language (Latin) that the story was originally written in.

Use the structure of the story to write a modern ghost story.

Write the scene in the house from the ghost's point of view.

Rewrite the story for a young audience, using the words discussed in the sentence level work above.

Prepare and perform a conversation between the philosopher and someone who doesn't believe in ghosts.

Year 6 activities

Word level

Use dictionaries to find meanings of difficult words and come up with personal definitions.

Use a dictionary to find and define other words beginning with *gh*.

Sentence level

Build complex sentences; rework the first paragraph into a single sentence.

Read the created sentence aloud for clarity of meaning.

Discuss the pronouns *his* and *it* in relation to the ghost. Why are both used?

Change some sentences into the passive voice – e.g. 'The spot was marked with a small pile of leaves.'
What effect does this have?

Revise previous work, particularly work on complex sentences, and use of punctuation.

Text level

Discuss how effective the narrative is in telling an exciting story. If it is deemed unexciting discuss what the author could do to make it more exciting.

Discuss whether direct speech would improve the story.

Discuss the role of the narrator. How did Pliny hear the story? Was it 'first hand' from the philosopher? Did he hear it as gossip? How might the story have changed in the telling? How does Pliny use detail to make the story more realistic?

Discuss an alternative ending to the story, perhaps involving a different discovery in the courtyard, the return of an even angrier ghost, or the appearance of a second ghost.

Group work and individual writing

Find other stories and poems involving ghosts.

Prepare a newspaper account of the haunting.

Rewrite the story, involving two ghosts rather than one.

Imagine that the ghost is, in fact, a hoax! Write an account from the hoaxer's point of view, explaining why and how the plan was carried out.

Use the story as the basis for poetry writing.

King Midas

Year 3 activities

Word level

Focus on spelling of *beautiful, surrounded, delighted, liquid, extravagant, whisper, busy, immediately, fabulous.*

Infer the meaning of difficult words from context.

Discuss the meaning of *extravagant* and collect synonyms and antonyms.

Focus on the *le* spelling as in *terrible*; compare with *petal*.

Build words from *hunger – hungry* (with dropped *e*) and *thirst – thirsty*.

Look at adding *ing* to verbs in die – dying.

Talk about the superlative *richest* and compare with *rich, richer*.

Talk about the prefix *dis* in *disappeared* and suffix *ful* in *wonderful, beautiful*.
Form *delightful* from *delight*, pointing out the single l.

Sentence level

Collect verbs and talk about their meaning – *loved, offered, touched, turned, realised*, etc.

Talk about speech marks and their function. For each example of their use, discuss who was talking to whom.

Collect adjectives: *beautiful, wonderful, fabulous, gleaming, flowing, liquid, terrible*. Form adjectives from *glittered, disappeared*, by adding *ing*, and *ashamed – shameful*, adding *ful*.

Find an adjective to qualify *king* in the sentence 'The gods hoped . . . '

Discuss singular and plural in relation to: *petal, rose*, and *garden*, and *furniture* which cannot be pluralised.

Identify pronouns: *he, his, them*.

Note capitalisation of proper nouns.

Text level

Look at the way paragraphing is used for direct speech.

Retell the main points of the story.

Discuss the character of Midas.

Discuss why Dionysus agreed to Midas's request.

Group work and individual writing

Present the story of Midas as a storyboard.

Write the dialogue between Midas and barber when a) The barber first sees the king's ears and b) when Midas discovers that the barber has revealed the secret.

Write an extended description of Midas's palace and gardens from imagination.

Write or improvise a conversation about Midas between Dionysus and Apollo.

Write a modern 'Midas' story.

Year 4 activities

Word level

Work on spellings of double consonant words – *begged, disappeared, glittered, cutting, passing.*

Discuss more interesting words in place of *good, busy, tired, chair, gift, hid.*

Understand contractions using an apostrophe – *didn't.*

Sentence level

Talk about commonly used expressions such as 'teach him a lesson', 'sworn to secrecy'.

Identify adverbs: *immediately, instantly.*

Rewrite the sentence:
'Midas spent a busy morning' using the adverb 'busily'.

Identify words and phrases that signal time sequences, e.g. *one day, at first, at last, soon, very soon.*

Understand the use of the apostrophe to show possession in *donkey's*, and *Midas's*. Talk about the use of the apostrophe for words ending in s.

Talk about the use of the comma in the sentence 'Soon the reeds grew . . .'

Text level

Talk about story structure, and note that the text is really two stories linked by a single main character.

Discuss the humour of the story. Discuss a new title for the extract that conveys the 'moral' of the Midas story.

Find words to characterise Apollo in this story.

Group work and individual writing

Write a character sketch of King Midas.

Write the first part of the story from the point of view of Midas, using the first person.

Write an entry for Midas's diary from the day he discovers he has a donkey's ears.

Write part of the story as a playscript. This could start at the point where Midas feels hungry and thirsty.

Discuss and write an alternative ending for either part of the story.

Year 5 activities

Word level

Look at the *ou* letter string in: *touched, although, colour*, and talk about the different pronunciation.

Revise work on the possessive apostrophe, and the apostrophe used for contraction.

Sentence level

Discuss rewriting sections of direct speech into indirect speech.

Discuss rewriting the text as a picture book for younger children. What changes would need to be made?

Practise reading aloud complex sentences with appropriate intonation.

Discuss use of the present tense in direct speech.

Discuss the use of the imperative in *let, bring*.

Identify prepositions: *on, under, over* etc.

Text level

List words used to describe the character of Midas. Discuss how we learn about him from his actions, and from what is said about him.

Find out about Dionysus and Apollo; read further Greek legends involving them.

Discuss what the 'moral' of each part of the story might be.

In some versions of the story, Midas touches his own child, who turns to gold. Discuss where this would fit in to the story and how it might be written.

Group work and individual writing

Write a newspaper account of either or both parts of the story, including a sensational 'tabloid' headline.

Rewrite the first part of the story from the point of view of Midas.

Write an additional scene in which Midas touches his own child.

Year 6 activities

Word level

Revise spellings of difficult words.

Collect words with internal *qu* spelling.

Build words from 'shame' – such as *ashamed, shamed, shameful, shameless,* and discuss the meaning.

Use a thesaurus for words similar in meaning to 'glittered'. Discuss their meaning.

Sentence level

Change selected sentences from active to passive, discussing how the meaning and form have changed.

Join shorter sentences together by using connectives.

Discuss the use of the exclamation mark in the text.

Text level

Talk about how the fairly plain telling of the story could be made more interesting and exciting, by use of extended description, more direct speech, or use of simile and metaphor.

Read further Greek myths; discuss their original language and how stories can change and adapt through the oral tradition.

Look up and read other versions of the Midas story and see how the details differ.

Discuss whether the story might be based on fact in any way, and how it might have changed since it was first told.

Group work and individual writing

Rewrite the story in précis form using less than a hundred words.

Use part of the story as stimulus for poetry writing.

Write a letter from the barber to Midas confessing what he has done and begging for mercy.

Design a poster for a film based on the Midas story, with appropriate text to persuade people to watch it.

Based on their understanding of Midas as a character, ask groups to plan further adventures in which he gets some sort of 'come-uppance' at the end.

The biggest turnip in the world

Year 3 activities

Word level

Investigate the spelling of verbs ending in *ing* – *come, coming; grow, growing.*

Identify words ending in *le – valuable, vegetable.*

Investigate *big, bigger, biggest.*

Infer or use a dictionary meaning of difficult words such as *unique.*

Discuss the difference between *valuable* and *expensive, remarkable* and *wonderful*, and *beautiful* and *magnificent.*

Investigate the use of the apostrophe in simple shortened forms – *let's, don't, I've, I'm.*

Sentence level

Identify the present tense as the most frequently used tense in play scripts.

Discuss the use of hyphen, question mark and exclamation mark, and read lines using them as guidance for correct emphasis and expression.

Text level

Gain understanding of the form of a play script, and the terms *dialogue, cast, stage directions, characters, scenes, script.* Learn that the spoken dialogue is printed differently from other words on the page.

Discuss the difference between a play script and speech set out in prose.

Gain awareness of different tones of voice and different registers – the difference between the brothers speaking with each other and with the queen. Discuss how the bracketed stage directions help with the performance of the lines.

Discuss the 'twist' at the end of the story and how the brothers might have felt about the outcome.

Discuss what makes the ending of the story funny.

Group work and individual writing

Write scene six, *Back at the farm* using the play script format.

Write the main points of the story in note form.

Year 4 activities

Word level

Investigate the use of the apostrophe in further contractions: *we'll, what's, here's.*

Discuss changes that would have to be made if there was a king rather than a queen.

Sentence level

Collect the words *remarkable, astonishing, wonderful.* Use knowledge of words and a thesaurus to find a range of synonyms. Discuss their meaning.

Investigate adverbs, particularly those used in stage directions – *excitedly, doubtfully.* Change 'In a respectful voice' to an adverb. Investigate whether *astonished* can form an adverb.

Identify possessive apostrophes in *Jack's, Queen's, world's.*

Text level

Discuss the chronology of the play: how much time may pass between the different scenes.

Discuss additional stage directions for lines that do not have them.

Discuss words to describe the characters of the two brothers.

Think of ways that Bill could have persuaded the Queen to give him something other than the turnip.

Think of an alternative title for the play that describes the brothers' situation at the end.

Discuss the idea of a 'moral' in stories, and the 'moral' behind this story. Was the behaviour of the brothers, or the queen, reasonable?

Discuss whether the queen guessed what the brothers were up to, and how she might have guessed.

Group work and individual writing

Discuss and work on an alternative scene 5.

Choose one scene and write an expanded version of it, with more extensive dialogue. (Each group could be given a different scene to expand.) Prepare a performance of the play with the new scene included.

Write an entry to the Queen's diary, in which she explained how clever she was to fool the farmers.

Year 5 activities

Word level

Find a range of words incorporating prefixes and suffixes, and identify their roots :
unusual, valuable, remarkable, wonderful.

Identify antonyms from the play that might be used to write *The World's Smallest Turnip.*

Sentence level

Discuss what words would have to be changed to make the story suitable for very young children.

Identify a line of dialogue that is not a complete sentence and discuss why this is permissible in a play script.

Join up sentences using connectives e.g. Jack's final line in scene 1. Discuss why short sentences are helpful for actors.

Text level

Find and read further stories by the Brothers Grimm, including the one this play was based on. Discuss differences between the play and the story, and the meaning of 'based on'.

Discuss how the farmers would speak in the presence of the Queen, and how the Queen would address them.

Discuss possible openings for a prose version of the story written in the third person.

Group work and individual writing

Plan out and write a prose version of the story.

Plan a poster for a performance of the play, including comments to attract the audience.

Write a newspaper account of the growing of the giant turnip.

Year 6 activities

Word level

Discuss the two meanings of the word *quite* –ie, *completely* (as in the extract) or *somewhat* (as in 'that's quite good'. Point out that 'unique' is a word that requires no qualification – 'somewhat unique' is meaningless – and that 'quite' in the extract is really redundant and is only used for emphasis.

Revisit and revise all previous word level work.

Sentence level

Identify a sentence that demonstrates the imperative. ('Use the money . . .') Discuss where else the imperative could have been used – if the Queen did not like the turnip, for example.

Identify and discuss the use of the conditional in 'If we're lucky . . .'

Text level

Discuss the structure of the play, gaining understanding of the 'twist' or surprise ending.

Discuss how actors use emphasis and inflection to reflect meaning.

Discuss the meaning of 'fairy tale' with reference to other writers such as Hans Christian Andersen.

Group work and individual writing

Plan, write and perform a version of the play in a modern setting, such as home or school, in which the plot is retained but the characters and 'props' are changed.

Prepare and run a storytelling session based on either the new or original version of the story, and perform it to a younger class.

Write brief character studies of the farmers.

Write a letter from the brothers to the Queen in which they apologise for their trick, explain that they are poor, and ask for their picture back.

Cider With Rosie

Year 3 activities

Word level

Discuss and gain understanding of the words *autobiography, bodily, bawling, rodeo, rabble, shrapnel, frizzed, hideous, plucked, gracious, boxed, smouldering.*

Use the dictionary when necessary to find meanings.

Discuss how the spelling of verbs alters when *ing* is added in *skating, skidding, stopping,* etc.

Discuss how the apostrophe is used to show shortened words.

Sentence level

Discuss the function of verbs and see how a simple past tense is formed by adding *–ed*. Discuss meaning of the verbs used and find synonyms.

Identify and discuss speech marks.

See how items in a list are demarcated by commas in the first sentence, and how this helps in the reading of the sentence.

Identify and discuss adjectives.

Learn that autobiographical writing is written in the first person.

Text level

Give an effective reading of the extract, demonstrating how non-standard orthography is used to show dialect and non-standard speech.

Discuss the misunderstanding at the end of the extract, and why Laurie Lee thought he was going to get a 'present'.

Talk about the humour in the passage. The experience was frightening for the young boy. Why do readers find it funny?

Understand that, although the extract is written like a story, it is factual writing.

Group work and individual writing

Discuss an interesting title for the extract.

Use the extract as a model for children's own writing on an early memory of school.

Write a short extension to the passage in which Laurie Lee's sisters explain why he is not going to get a present.

19

Year 4 activities

Word level

Identify and practise the spelling of words with double consonants, e.g. *ragged, skidding, stopping*.

Point out the silent letter in *wrapped*.

Discuss the word *overdoing* and find other words beginning with *over*.

Look at the compound word *playground* and create *play-* words and *-ground* words.

Discuss how Laurie Lee's nickname 'Loll' might have come about.

Sentence level

Revise work on using the past tense for narratives.

Look at the use of strong verbs such as *roared, plucked, screwed*, perhaps using cloze procedure.

Discuss the meaning of the adverb *fatly*.

Discuss Laurie Lee's use of figurative language in 'roared like a rodeo', 'spun me round like a top', 'grit like …shrapnel'.

Identify and name common punctuation marks.

Text level

Identify clues that suggest the text is not set in the present day.

Discuss the differences between Laurie Lee's school and schools today.

Understand the meaning of the word *simile* and discuss its use in the passage.

Discuss the use of 'incorrect' speech and the contrast between this and the formally correct writing of the rest of the passage.

Discuss why Laurie didn't take his sister's threat seriously.

Group work and individual writing

Perform the two sections of direct speech as a 'mini' two-act play.

Write a short character sketch of Laurie Lee as he appears in this extract.

Rewrite the first section of speech in standard English.

Year 5 activities

Word level

Discuss the irregular plural in *scarf/scarves* and find other examples e.g. *half/halves, calf/calves*.

Revise doubling of consonants after short vowels in *skid/skidding, wrap/wrapping*.

Revise unusual vocabulary such as *hideous, shrapnel*, etc.

Sentence level

Discuss unusual and figurative use of adjectives in *hideous, smouldering*.

Introduce the concept of metaphor.

Point out how the direct speech dispenses with phrases such as 'I said' apart from at the very beginning of the extract, and discuss the effect this has on the liveliness of the passage.

Revise work on the setting out of direct speech.

Identify prepositions e.g. *through, on*.

Text Level

Work on a dramatised reading of the extract.

Discuss the effect on the passage of the use of imagery and unusual vocabulary.

Group work and individual writing

Rewrite part of the playground scene in the present tense, e.g. 'skate and skim around me', 'The rabble are closing in . . . '. Discuss the effect this has.

Write an imaginative description of Laurie Lee's arrival in the playground in the third person.

Rewrite the final section of direct speech into reported speech and discuss the effect this has.

Year 6 activities

Word level

Discuss the various meanings of the word *present*, and how the confusion over meaning gives the extract its joke.

Study the words used metaphorically and find interesting alternatives.

Sentence level

Starting at 'Old boots, ragged stockings…' use connectives to rework the remainder of the paragraph into two sentences. Discuss a range of ways to achieve this.

Discuss Laurie Lee's use of the colon, semi-colon, and dashes.

Discuss how use of 'incorrect' English in the dialogue such as 'I'm stopping 'ome' and 'get chopped up Sundays' adds to the liveliness of the passage. What would the effect be of 'correcting' the passage?

Review the conventions of recounting and autobiographical writing.

Text level

Discuss how Laurie Lee manages to write from the point of view of a young child.

Compare Laurie Lee's account of a first day at school with that of other writers, e.g. Roger McGough in his poem *First Day At School*.

Discuss how unpleasant experiences do not seem so bad in retrospect and how people can find humour in looking back on childhood experiences.

Read and discuss further extracts from *Cider With Rosie*.

Group work and individual writing

Find other writing by Laurie Lee, such as his poetry. Find out some information about him.

Write a poem based on the extract, selecting interesting words and images for inclusion.

Write an account of Laurie's experience in the playground from the point of view of the young teacher or one of the other children.

Let me persuade you!

Year 3 activities

Word level

Discuss vocabulary such as *persuade, environment, competing, designer, malls.*

Identify and learn spelling patterns such as *le* ending in *example, tion* in *station,* double consonants in *smelly, swimming.*

Build on *easy* to make *easier, easiest.*

Discuss compound words – *airport, seaside, countryside.*

Discuss the use of the apostrophe to shorten words in *you're, it's.*

Sentence level

Practise reading aloud sections of the text using punctuation as a guide.

Identify and list verbs.

Discuss the use of question and exclamation marks in the passage.

Identify adjectives, and understand the term. Find alternatives to *big.*

Discuss the use of the comma in the sentence beginning 'People think cities are . . . '

Discuss the use of the first person for opinions – 'I think that . . .' and the second person for instructions 'You can go to . . .'

Identify singular and plural nouns.

Text level

Discuss whether the passage is fact or fiction.

Find key points in the extract and summarise the argument.

Talk about the use of numbers and bullet points to organise the extract.

Discuss with the class whether they agree with Sanjay.

Group work and individual writing

Ask groups to make a list of five key things that make cities attractive places to live.

Make a further list for the countryside.

Write a short account of a visit to one of the attractions listed by Sanjay.

Design a poster for a city to encourage visitors. This could be general, or specific to a city they know.

Year 4 activities

Word level

Identify the homophones: *there, they're, their,* and discuss the different meanings.

Discuss *ing* ending in *complaining, competing*.

Discuss the construction of the word *beautiful,* and find other words with the suffix.

Discuss the pluralisation of *city* to make *cities*. Find other words that follow this construction.

Sentence level

Identify the adverb *really* and discuss its function in qualifying the adjective *good*. Find other adverbs that could be used to indicate intensity – *quite, fairly, very, extremely*.

Ensure understanding of the word 'tense' and discuss why this form of writing requires the use of the present tense.

Discuss how the fifth paragraph could be rewritten to avoid use of the question.

Text level

Discuss in detail the purpose of the text and how the layout is used to support this.

Discuss how effectively Sanjay uses paragraphs.

For each paragraph discuss a possible single-word heading instead of the number, e.g. *environment, friends,* etc.

Discuss what is fact and which opinion.

Group work and individual writing

Create a concept map showing the key features of city life.

Using the structure of the passage, choose a different place – the countryside, a village, the seaside, for example – and present arguments for living there. This could extend into fantasy writing – the moon, a distant planet, the bottom of the sea.

Write a letter to Sanjay disagreeing with him.

Year 5 activities

Word level

Identify the *–side* construction in *seaside, countryside*. Find other examples such as *riverside, lakeside*, *'stateside'* (America) *downside, topside*. Create new words such as *Cityside*.

Sentence level

Discuss use of auxiliary verbs *could*, *would*, in the conditional mood ('I would soon get lonely if . . . you would go . . .')

Text level

Discuss the effectiveness of the opening and closing sentences.

Discuss use of persuasive language such as 'you must agree . . .'.

Discuss the use of hypothetical construction in 'If you want . . . ' 'If you live . . . '

Group work and individual writing

Extend Sanjay's list of city attractions.

Write additional sentences using the conditional construction beginning with *if*. These can be formed into a nonsense poem:

If pigeons ate nothing but jelly,
they would wobble through the sky

If badgers ate nothing but ice-cream,
they would turn into polar bears . . .

Prepare a set of notes based on Sanjay's ideas. This could take the form of a list with headings and subheadings, or a concept map.

Year 6 activities

Word level

Discuss newly coined words and phrases such as: *designer clothes, shopping malls, recreation centres.*

Make a list of other new words and phrases that apply to cities, e.g. *pedestrian precinct, burger bar,* and their (mostly American) origin.

Sentence level

Discuss the use of clauses beginning with the word *because* (adverbial clause of reason). Construct further sentences based on the extract using such a clause, e.g. Parks are better than the countryside because . . .

Text level

Discuss how Sanjay manages to achieve a relaxed, informal tone to his writing. Rewrite some sentences in a more formal style and discuss the differences.

Discuss how effective Sanjay's arguments are and where he has used deliberate exaggeration to make his point.

Group work and individual writing

Imagine Sanjay is to visit the class. In note form, prepare a series of questions that could be put to him to make him justify his point of view.

Write a piece of persuasive writing using this passage as a model. This could be on an environmental issue, or any other topic the writer feels strongly about. The writing should be logical and effective, pre-empting counter arguments and clearly indicating the writer's point of view.

Letter from Mrs Stevenson

Year 3 activities

Word level

Discuss unusual vocabulary such as: *voyage, deathly, weevils, yeast, molasses, midst, matted, administer, restoratives*, using a dictionary or, where possible, inferring their meaning from the context.

Discuss the meaning of *wonderfully* and break it down into its parts. Construct further words based on *wonder*.

Discuss the meaning of *etc*.

Sentence level

Discuss the format of the letter and the use of the second person – 'You could hardly believe . . .' in the first paragraph.

Show how the punctuation in the last two sentences guides the way it is read.

Identify and discuss adjectives, especially those used in unexpected ways.

Text level

Ensure understanding of some of the difficult phrases in the passage – e.g. 'To keep house on a yacht is no easy thing'.

Discuss the feelings of Fanny Stevenson
a at sea and
b on land.

Which does she prefer and why? What words does she use to describe her feelings?

Discuss why Fanny Stevenson did not want to talk to the cook.

Discuss why a letter is written mainly in the first person.

Talk about how Fanny Stevenson manages to make her letter 'chatty' and informal.

Group work and individual writing

Write a modern letter from someone on a sea voyage explaining the problems of life at sea. How would such a letter be set out? What address could be used to head the letter?

Make a list of the duties of the 'lady of the yacht'. What else might she have to do?

Year 4 activities

Word level

Look at *–ly* constructions – *wonderfully, hardly, deathly, really.*

Use alternative expressions for difficult expressions such as: *deathly sea-sick, pretty high, cracked head, dress the wound,* etc.

Discuss construction of words ending in *ing*, e.g. *thinking, lying, clutching.*

Discuss the *ous* ending in *delicious, dangerous,* and find other words with this ending from elsewhere.

Discuss any words that seem old-fashioned, e.g. *amongst, cares.*

Sentence level

Discuss the non-standard punctuation and sentence formation, and the effect of changing into more standard English.

Form adverbs from words in the passage, e.g. *deliciously, prettily, heavily.*

Discuss the function of the adverbs in the passage, e.g. *wonderfully.*

Find examples of past and present tense in the passage.

Discuss the use of the apostrophe to show possession.

Text level

Ensure full understanding of expressions used in the letter: e.g. what does 'Louis has improved' tell us about him, and 'I have more cares than I was really fit for' tell us about Mrs Stevenson?

Find out more about Robert Louis Stevenson – see teachers' notes on *Treasure Island*, page 3. Find any poems by him (such as those from *A Child's Garden of Verses*) that show how important travel was to him.

Group work and individual writing

Write a correctly set out letter to Fanny Stevenson asking about the voyage and her adventures in the South Seas.

Write an exciting account of the 'dangerous weather', explaining how the mate cracked his head.

Year 5 activities

Word level

Collect synonyms for words such as *deathly, high, directions, dangerous*.

Discuss the unusual use of words such as *delicious, deathly, high*.

Sentence level

Discuss the words of the cook. Is this direct speech, or a list of the sort of questions the cook asks?

Discuss how quotation marks are used in 'Lady of the yacht'.

Show how Fanny Stevenson's use of the commas help in understanding, perhaps by writing out the sentence beginning 'In the midst of dangerous weather' without punctuation.

Revise the use of the apostrophe to show possession.

Text level

Discuss a range of purposes for letters and the level of formality required.

Discuss various letter openings and conclusions, e.g. Dear sir or madam, Dear Mike, yours faithfully, love from, and so on. Discuss which of these is appropriate for various contexts.

Group work and individual writing

Write a character sketch of Fanny Stevenson as she appears in her letter.

Write a letter from Robert Louis Stevenson to a friend in which he describes all the things his wife does as 'Lady of the yacht'.

Year 6 activities

Word level

Look for and collect archaic use of words and expressions, e.g. *must needs, restoratives*.

Discuss the colloquial use of the word 'pretty'.

Sentence level

Discuss how Fanny Stevenson makes use of the present tense to make her description come to life.

Discuss why the sentence starting 'It was when I was deathly sea-sick' is not really a sentence at all, and why this is permissible in an informal letter.

Text level

Discuss how Mrs Stevenson made her letter amusing for her friend.

Group work and individual writing

Improvise and perform the scene when the ship's cook seeks advice from a sea-sick Mrs Stevenson.

Produce a modern version of Fanny Stevenson's letter.

Write a short section of a biography of Fanny Stevenson, describing her experiences on the yacht.

TWO DIARIES

Year 3 activities

Word level

Discuss difficult and unusual vocabulary, e.g. *waterside, barges, hovered, singlet, toddled, survey, deposited, substantial*.

Formation of words with the *ing* suffix – *burning, trying, flinging, carrying, hugging, scanning, surrounding*.

Practise spelling of *igh* words – *night, eighteen, delightful, fighters*.

Sentence level

Identify verbs and look for synonyms for *got, went*, and *stayed* in the Pepys extract.

Discuss the function of verbs and see how a simple past tense is formed by adding *ed*.

Find adjectives that describe quality or degree – *great, terrible, delightful, terrific, amazing* – and suggest alternatives.

Identify singular and plural nouns.

Discuss the use of capitals for proper nouns.

Find words and expressions that show time passing – *soon, had just – when, then, after a few moments*.

Text level

Discuss the historical context of the two extracts. Look for points of similarity and ask why the passages have been paired together. Ensure that it is understood that these extracts are non-fiction.

Discuss the purpose of diaries and the difference between an 'appointments' diary and a journal.

Understand the meaning of a chronological report and discuss the time-scale of each passage.

Discuss what Colin might keep in his briefcase that is so important to him. What would members of the class try to save in the event of an air-raid?

Group work and individual writing

Use the information in one of the passages as the basis of a story written in the first person.

Rewrite the first paragraph of the Pepys extract using either direct speech or play script form. Expand with additional ideas – was Pepys annoyed about being woken up?

Write a page of a real or imaginary diary.

Year 4 activities

Word level

Discuss the differences between *amazing* and *fascinating*, and *terrible* and *terrific*.

Identify and practise the spelling of words with double consonants.

Discuss the meaning of informal words 'toddled' and 'popped' in Colin Perry's extract.

Pepys uses the word 'poor' twice in his extract. What meaning does the word have in each case? What other words could be used?

Discuss formation of words with the *ed* suffix, e.g. *stayed, accompanied, presented, fancied*.

Sentence level

Practise reading aloud longer sentences, using punctuation as a guide.

Revise work on using the past tense for narratives.

Find examples of the use of the present tense in the Colin Perry extract.

Discuss the meaning of the phrase 'most assuredly'.

Text level

Discuss how both authors use small details to bring their accounts to life, e.g. the description of the pigeons in Pepys's diary, and the details of family life in the Colin Perry extract.

Discuss which passage is the most exciting.

Talk about Colin Perry's own feelings about the bombing – is he more excited than frightened? Why?

Discuss anything strange or inconsistent about the Colin Perry extract, e.g. why was he eating Sunday lunch in his underwear? Why does he say that he returned to 'cold chicken' at the end of the extract after telling us that he 'finished his dinner' in the previous sentence?

Group work and individual writing

Choose one extract and prepare a newspaper front page using information from the extract.

Work on imaginative accounts of disasters, e.g. a meteorite impact, a fire, a plane crash.

Collect ideas and images from the extracts and use them as the basis of poetry writing.

31

Year 5 activities

Word level

Discuss the word *belongings* and find others words using the *ings* suffix – *leavings, sweepings, savings*. Discuss what these words have in common.

Revise doubling of consonants after short vowels.

Discuss possible alternatives for *delightful, toddled, hugging, deposited, commencement, popped*.

Collect words connecting with seeing and discuss their meaning, e.g. *survey, scanning, spectacle, showed, noticed*. Add to the list from other texts or a thesaurus. Make a 'mini-dictionary' for these words. Find substitutes for 'saw' and 'noticed' in the Pepys extract.

Discuss the meaning of the word *sweeping* in the Colin Perry extract.

Sentence level

Some of the sentences in the Colin Perry extract are ambiguous, e.g. 'Putney too appeared to have been hit, but it may have been a factory chimney'. Discuss these ambiguities and suggest ways that the sentences could be made clearer.

Discuss the use of auxiliary verbs such as *were, was, had*, in both extracts. Discuss the effect of changing the verbs, e.g. *roared* instead of *were roaring*, and how this can make the writing more powerful.

Text level

Talk about Colin Perry's answer to Davis in the final paragraph. Who might Davis be? Is Colin Perry's answer a sensible one? What does he mean by 'That is good enough for him'?

Colin Perry seems more concerned with his dinner getting cold than with the destruction caused by the bombs! Is this a fair comment? What does Pepys say in his diary (first paragraph) that suggests that he too is concerned about his own property?

Group work and individual writing

Discuss how Pepys could make his account more exciting. What words and phrases from Colin Perry's account could be used for this? Use this idea for a rewrite of the Pepys extract.

Write (or improvise) the scene in the shelter with Davis and Colin's parents trying to persuade Colin not to return to the flat.

Year 6 activities

Word level

From Colin Perry's diary, collect words specifically linked with the second world war e.g. *air-raid, dive-bombers, hostilities, shelter, raiders, all-clear, Nazis.*

Sentence level

Identify the use of indirect speech in both extracts, and discuss what words were actually spoken.

Discuss how Colin Perry uses the present tense in his writing. What effect does this have?

Text level

Colin Perry says he went down to the shelter 'for the sake of my parents'. What does he mean by this?

Discuss Colin Perry's simile of the swarm of bees. Why is this effective?

Discuss Colin Perry's attitude to the war. How might this differ from that of his parents? How does it differ from Pepys's attitude to the fire?

Discuss which extract is the most exciting. How does the author achieve this?

Group work and individual writing

Discuss what Davis actually said to Colin Perry, then write their conversation using direct speech.

Write a character sketch of Colin Perry based on the extract.

Rewrite Pepys's account of the pigeons or the people rescuing their belongings, using an interesting and appropriate simile.

Improvise an 'on the spot' TV report for either extract.

Report on Planet 4

Year 3 activities

Word level

Collect and understand new vocabulary, particularly technical words such as *canyon, atmosphere, probes, diameter, Celsius*.

Recognise the prefix *un* – in *manned, unmanned, likely, unlikely*.

Sentence level

Locate and discuss capitalised words – *Earth, Mars, Phobos*, etc.

Read out sentences correctly using punctuation to guide the sense.

Discuss how descriptive writing uses predominantly the present tense.

Collect adjectives and discuss synonyms that could be used in their place.

Find sentences that can be joined using connectives.

Text level

Before reading the passage, discuss what the class would like to find out about the planet Mars.

After reading, see how many have been answered and what the class would still like to know.

Before reading the whole text, look at the subheadings and discuss what each paragraph is likely to cover.

After reading through the text, close the book and ask the class what key information they have remembered.

Ask the class which aspects of the information they found most interesting and what they would like further information on, or like to know more about.

Questions to test understanding: Why is it cold on Mars? Why is it not suitable for life? Why would it take years for a manned mission to reach it?

Group work and individual writing

Discuss and make notes on the key things the group has learnt about the planet Mars.

Write an extract from the diary of the first person on Mars.

Use this plan to write an account of an imaginary planet, using appropriate subheadings.

Year 4 activities

Word level

Discuss double consonants in *unmanned, mission, million*.

Collect words for size, starting with *huge, vast*.

Discuss individual meanings.

Look at homophones *two, too, to*.

Discuss the use of figures in the extract – use of words for small numbers (two) and figures for larger numbers (228).

Sentence level

Identify adverb *simply*. Suggest further adverb to qualify *sweep*.

Form comparatives and superlatives from *further, high, thin, deep*.

Discuss the conjunction *so* and its use in the second paragraph.

Text level

Discuss the arrangement of material into paragraphs.

Summarise orally the content of each paragraph in one sentence.

Discuss the opening paragraph and its function.

Attempt to replace paragraph headings with a single word.
(Or two using the definite/indefinite article.)

Group work and individual writing

Use other resource materials, including the Internet, to collect further information on Mars.

Make a list of key words from the passage.

Write two paragraphs making the case for and against life on Mars.

Write a newspaper account of the first landing on Mars.

Present the information in the final paragraph in pictorial form, i.e. with planets of different sizes, illustration of two thermometers, etc.

Year 5 activities

Word level

Discuss alternatives that could replace *scientist*, e.g. *astronomer, geologist, biologist*. Discuss the specific fields of knowledge of these scientists.

Discuss the words *volcano/volcanoes*, making a list of other words ending in *o* and seeing how the plural form is formed.

Introduce the word *uninhabitable* and discuss whether it applies to the planet Mars. Break the word down into its component parts to see how it is constructed.

Sentence level

Discuss words and phrases used to make comparisons, e.g. *while, compared with, than, almost the same, nearly twice as*.

Talk about what would have to be changed to present the information to a younger audience.

Discuss the various forms of paragraph headings, i.e. asking a question, quoting from the paragraph, summarising the paragraph.

Introduce the phrases 'main heading' and 'sub heading' and ensure they are understood.

Text level

Discuss the key words from a selected paragraph.

Discuss how the information in the final paragraph might be better presented as a table, graph, or illustration.

Group work and individual writing

Present the information in the final paragraph in a variety of forms, e.g. a two-column table, charts, and graphs.

Construct an argument for and against manned exploration of the planet Mars.

Year 6 activities

Word level

Work on dictionary definitions for some of the technical words in the extract.

Investigate the origins of the names Mars, Phobos, Deimos. Extend this to the names of other planets and satellites.

Sentence level

Rearrange sentences in different ways to see how meaning and punctuation will change, e.g. 'Some scientists believe that, deep down under the surface . . .'

Change the sentence 'Vast dust storms . . .' into the passive, beginning 'The planet is . . .'

Text level

Differentiate known facts – 'Mars is 228 kilometres from the sun' – from facts that are not fully confirmed – 'there are signs that' – and supposition – 'there may have been' . . . 'there may still be'.

Discuss the difficulties of manned trips to Mars, and the ways in which people are better than robots in exploring unknown places.

Group activity and individual writing

Prepare questions that might feature in a 'SATs' exam paper on the planet Mars. These can be simple, factual questions –
'how far . . . ?'
or more complex ones:
'What are the arguments for and against life on Mars?'

Write and perform a 'live interview' with the first person to land on Mars. This can come direct from Mars, or can take place on the astronaut's return.

Using the model of the Mars text, write a report on another planet.

Write a report written by an alien visitor on the planet Earth.

AN EXPLANATION

How does a mobile phone work?

Year 3 activities

Word level

This passage contains a good deal of technical vocabulary. Talk through and explore meanings of these words:

handset, transmitter, receiver, electronic, rechargeable, keypad, Internet, signal, cellular.

Look at prefixes *in – incoming*, and *re–reconnect*. Form other words using these prefixes – *inward, inshore, rewind, redial, revisit.*

Sentence level

Understand new words such as *update, location,* by breaking them down into component parts and looking at their grammatical context.

Identify verbs and discuss how the present tense is used almost exclusively in explanatory writing.

See how numbers are used to show a sequence of events or instructions.

Collect and discuss the meaning of adjectives in the text, e.g. *powerful, complex.*

Talk through more complex sentences such as 'If your phone is switched off . . .' looking at the use of connectives and punctuation.

Text level

Discuss before reading the passage what the class knows about mobile phones and what questions they would like to ask. After reading, discuss how many questions have been answered.

Look at the three paragraphs and sum each one up in a word or short phrase, e.g. introduction, the handset, the network.

Make a list of key words and phrases from the text.

Talk about the various parts of the handset (display screen, send key, end call key, receive key) and their function.

Group work and individual writing

Write a simple series of numbered notes explaining how to make a call on a mobile phone, e.g:
1 switch on the phone
2 check for battery and signal
3 key in the number . . .

Design a simple flow chart showing a mobile phone network.

Draw a diagram of a mobile phone handset. This can be based on the information in the passage, the pupil's own experience, or using imagination.

Write a list of advantages of a mobile phone compared with a standard 'fixed' phone. If possible, include disadvantages (cost, need to recharge batteries, etc).

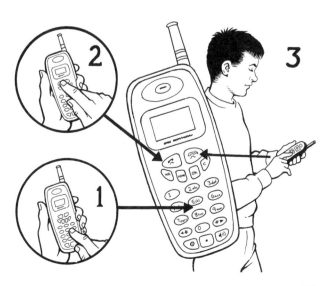

Year 4 activities

Word level

Discuss technical words and phrases such as *complex electronic package, key in, carry out functions, access, memory* (in its electronic sense), *text message, on line, charge, identification, call centre.*

List and check spelling of double consonant words, e.g. *transmitter, called, possible.*

Build words based on *call* and discuss meanings, e.g. *caller, calling*, and phrases such as *call centre, call waiting.*

Look at the use of *cc* in *access* and find other words using these letters, e.g. *success.*

Sentence level

Discuss the use of the word 'even' in the first paragraph and its purpose.

Identify words and phrases in the second paragraph that show a time sequence.

Suggest alternative titles for the text to change it from a question, e.g. How a mobile phone works, Your mobile phone explained, Using a mobile phone. Look also for snappier titles such as Get mobile!

Rewrite the sentence beginning 'Making a call involves. . .' using
1 commas and
2 bullet points
instead of the numbers. What has been lost?

Text level

Summarise orally the content of the main paragraphs, beginning 'This paragraph explains . . .'

Discuss and understand what is meant by explanatory text, and how it differs from other forms of non-fiction.

Look at examples of 'cause and effect' – if . . . then . . .

Find examples of the passive voice – the 'receive call button is pressed'.

Discuss other ways that the information in the text could be presented, such as a labelled diagram.

Group work and individual writing

Design a labelled diagram of a handset with captions that explain the various functions.

Use the format of the text to explain the function and use of a further piece of equipment, e.g.. a standard telephone, a fax machine, a hand-held computer game.

Year 5 activities

Word level

Discuss the meaning of *complex* as an adjective and a noun and how it differs from *complicated*.

Revise technical words from the passage.

Sentence level

Discuss the use of quotation marks in the passage.

Discuss the meaning of 'more correctly' at the beginning of the second paragraph and find a simpler way of expressing the meaning of this sentence.

Text level

Discuss how the second paragraph would need to be changed for use with a much younger audience.

Discuss how the first paragraph could be changed into instructional writing by use of the imperative, e.g. Make a call by . . .

Discuss how the passage might be written by a future archaeologist digging up a mobile phone, e.g. . . . handset was a powerful . . . A keypad enabled . . .

Group work and individual writing

Prepare and write a simple illustrated guide to a mobile phone for young children.

Write a section of the archaeologist's report suggested under text level work.

Design a poster or advertising brochure for a mobile phone, stressing advantages over standard phones and simplicity of use.

Year 6 activities

Word level

Look at the origin of the word 'dial' and discuss why it is still used today.

Discuss recently coined words and expressions such as *Internet, on line*.

Discuss the contemporary use of the word *package*.

Consider the word *telephone*. What is its origin? Why is the shortened form more often used?

Sentence level

Discuss the differences in approach in the two main paragraphs; in particular, note that the second is written in the second person while the first is written impersonally in the third person.

Discuss what changes would have to be made to write the first paragraph in the second person – 'A keypad enables you . . .' and the second paragraph in the third person – 'When the phone is switched on . . .'
What is gained by writing in the second person?

Text level

Point out and discuss the key features of explanatory text:
- impersonal writing,
- the use of technical terms,
- cause and effect constructions – 'if . . . then',
- chronological sequences – 'when . . . it . . . then . . .'

Point out the use of the future tense in constructions such as 'It will send . . .'.

Discuss the changes brought about by mobile phones, and the objections that some people have to them.

Group work and individual writing

Write a short explanatory account of operating a simple device, first impersonally, then in the second person.

Produce a persuasive piece of writing entitled 'I hate mobile phones!'

Write a letter to a wealthy aunt or uncle explaining why a mobile phone would be an ideal birthday present.

39

DISCUSSION
Travelling to school

Year 3 activities

Word level

Collect and understand new vocabulary such as *congestion, pollution, environment, efficient, convenience*.

Discuss the use of the apostrophe to shorten words such as: *can't, isn't*.

Collect and practise spelling of words with *tion* endings: *congestion, pollution, option*.

Sentence level

Read out sentences correctly using punctuation to guide the sense.

Collect adjectives and discuss synonyms that could be used in their place.

Find sentences that can be joined using connectives.

Identify verbs and discuss how the present tense is used almost exclusively in putting forward points of view.

Discuss how bullet points are used to emphasise non-chronological points.

Text level

Discuss the issue raised in the topic before reading the passage; after reading discuss how well the arguments were predicted.

Identify the key issues on both sides of the argument.

Discuss the meaning of 'compromise'.

Group work and individual writing

Carry out a group survey of means of coming to school. Collect reasons why this method is chosen.

Rework the information in the passage as a simple 'for and against' chart.

Work on a piece of descriptive writing on 'outside our school at 8.45 am'. This can be real or imaginary.

Year 4 activities

Word level

Identify *–ing* words such as *walking, travelling, pouring, belonging* and discuss their spelling. Form other *–ing* words from words in the passage.

Identify the adverb *increasingly*. Suggest an appropriate adverb for 'the roads are . . . congested'.

Sentence level

Identify possessive apostrophes for singular and plural words in *car's, parents'*.

Replace the dash in the sentence 'Children often have to carry . . .' with a suitable connective.

Discuss how the present tense is used in argumentative writing.

Look at and discuss the use of the colon to introduce lists.

Text level

Discuss the differences between fact and opinion.

Look at the opening paragraph and discuss how it is used to summarise the content of the passage.

Note the use of headings to introduce the two major points of view.

Discuss how persuasive the two arguments are.

Group work and individual writing

Write an imaginary newspaper report based on the extract: this could be an acount of a demonstration or protest, or a report on how a school has tackled the problem.

Write a list of rules for parents delivering pupils to school by car.

Discuss how information on how pupils come to school could be presented graphically.

Design a 'Walk to school' poster.

Year 5 activities

Word level

Discuss the meaning of phrases such as *rush hour, local residents*.

Discuss the meaning of the words *option* and *compromise*.

Discuss clichés and idiomatic expressions such as *choked with cars, dropped off*, and how the word *fine* is used idiomatically.

Sentence level

Further work on colons; discussion of the use of bullet points.

Revise the use of the present tense in non-fiction writing.

Identify and collect prepositions.

Discuss the use of the dash and think about connectives that could be used as alternatives to link clauses, such as *as, because, such as*.

Text level

Discuss and list 'key points' for each side of the argument.

Evaluate the arguments through discussion, adding additional points from local experience.

Discuss how persuasive the two arguments are .

Group work and individual writing

Prepare a letter to be sent to parents outlining the problems caused by cars and asking them to consider alternatives.

Write a fictional account of an incident outside the school involving parking problems in which people become annoyed.

Prepare a series of arguments for and against using a bicycle to come to school.

Year 6 activities

Word level

Discuss the figurative use of the word *choked*.

Discuss which words and expressions have entered the language or changed their meaning in recent years, e.g. *rush hour, the environment*.

Look at the compound word *driveway* and build others such as *roadway, clearway, railway, highway, superhighway*. Create new ones for the future such as *spaceway, starway*.

Sentence level

Work on combining shorter sentences into long ones by using connectives.

Look at the sentence beginning 'Children often have to . . .' and work on rewriting it using a standard sentence construction.

Rework the sentence beginning 'The great number of cars . . .' using conditionals such as *if . . . then, might, could, would*.

Discuss how the author of the extract uses an informal style to give readability.

Text level

Revise work on persuasive argument, looking at how the author sets out the information for each point of view. Discuss the idea of debate, where both sides of an argument are presented and a vote taken. Gain understanding of the expression *pros and cons*.

Discuss the differences between a compromise and a consensus.

Discuss if the final paragraph fairly sums up the view and offers a reasonable compromise.

Group work and individual writing

Choose another issue with clear 'pros and cons' and ask pupils to write about it using the passage as a model.

Hold a debate on the issues raised in the extract.

Discuss or write about why children in the past – say in Victorian times – found walking to school less of a problem than children today.

How to make a garden for a person with a visual handicap

Year 3 activities

Word level

Discuss difficult vocabulary in the extract: *visually, handicapped, environment, feature, aromatic, texture, flavour, flagstone.*

Locate and discuss words with an *le* ending: *possible, people, rustle, vegetable.*

Discuss the use of the apostrophe to shorten words such as *don't.*

Sentence level

Discuss meanings of words such as *sources, install, feature, texture,* using the context of the passage.

Look for redundancy in the paragraph on sound by deleting words one at a time.

Read out sentences correctly using punctuation to guide the sense.

Talk about adjectives such as *interesting* and *attractive* and look for alternatives.

Text level

Talk about why the term *visual handicap* is used rather than the word 'blind', i.e. many people are partially sighted.

Before reading the passage discuss the title and ask children to come up with their own ideas, or predict what suggestions will be made. After reading see how many ideas were covered and what ideas the passage did not include.

Look at the structure of the passage: main headings, sub-headings, and sub-sub-headings.

Talk about the meaning of an instructional text and to think about other types such as recipes, operating instructions, sets of rules.

Group work and individual writing

Use the form of the text for a piece of instructional writing, e.g. how to care for an animal, how to grow sunflowers.

Use the text draw up a list of 'do's and don'ts' for a garden for a visually handicapped person. Use bullet points for each 'do' and 'don't'.

Make notes from memory of the key points of the text.

Year 4 activities

Word level

Collect double consonant words: *possible, better, attractive, different, rubbed.*

Make a dictionary of texture words that might apply to the garden, starting with *rough* and *smooth.*

Look at compound words: *footpath, handrails, flagstones.*
Think of others beginning with *foot* or *hand.*

Make a dictionary of plant words: *flowers, shrubs, herbs, trees, bushes, grasses, fruit, vegetables.*
Write a definition for each one.

Distinguish between *to / too / two.*

Sentence level

Identify verbs, and how they are used imperatively: *make, think about, don't forget, install,* and so on.
Make a list of verbs that might be used in a cookery recipe: *weigh, measure, mix, pour,* etc.

Talk about how sentences are joined with conjunctions such as *but, and.*

Form comparatives and superlatives from *safe, rough, smooth, fresh.*

Text level

Discuss the arrangement of material into paragraphs.

Summarise orally the content of each section.

Discuss the opening paragraph and its function.

Discuss why 'imperative' verbs are an important feature of instructional writing.

Discuss why the suggestions in the text are particularly suited for visually handicapped people – wide paths. handrails, no prickly plants, etc.

Group work and individual writing

Use the suggestions in the text to draw a plan of a garden for the visually handicapped.

Write a newspaper report on the creation of such a garden for use by the community. Include an interview with one of the garden users.

Produce a further piece of instructional writing, this time one that has a chronological structure.

Year 5 activities

Word level

Find and discuss plurals such as *grass/grasses, bush/bushes, leaf/leaves*.

Discuss the use of the apostrophe in *people's* and *don't*.
Explain that words like *children* and *people* take an apostrophe before the *s* to show possession.

Focus on spelling polysyllabic words with unstressed syllables, e.g. *environment, important, possible*.

Sentence level

Work on rewriting a sentence with a different arrangement, e.g.
- People with a visual handicap who want to enjoy . . .
- To enjoy their gardens people . . .
- A safe environment is needed if . . .

Discuss what words might be difficult for a very young audience and what substitutes could be made.

Collect and discuss prepositions such as *at, round, into, beneath*.

Practise reading aloud complex sentences such as the first in the passage, using the punctuation to guide the sense.

Text level

Before reading the text, discuss the issues involved and ask for suggestions. See how many of these ideas are included in the text.

Evaluate the organisation, layout and usefulness of the text.

Group work and individual writing

Rewrite the 'sound' paragraph using bullet points for each source of sound mentioned.

Design a poster or brochure encouraging visitors to the garden.

Write a 'diary account' from the point of view of a person with a visual handicap following a visit to the garden.

Create a concept map of the information contained within the passage.

Year 6 activities

Word level

Explore plant names and collect those that can be used as first names.

Revise unusual vocabulary such as *aromatic, visually, environment, texture*.

Sentence level

Revise the use of the conventions of instructional writing, such as the use of the imperative.

Link shorter sentences to make more complex ones using connectives.

Text level

Discuss how the information in the extract might be useful in different contexts, e.g. within the school.

Discuss how an indoor attraction such as a museum could be designed with visually handicapped people in mind.

Group work and individual writing

Rewrite one paragraph in the first person, from the point of view of the gardener:

I hung wind chimes, and looked for . . .

Discuss and write about how other places could be adapted for a visually handicapped person, e.g. a kitchen.

Use the plan and layout of the extract to give instructions for a different task such as building a safe environment for a pet.

A recipe for kedgeree

Year 3 activities

Word level

Discuss new vocabulary: *ingredients: haddock, parsley, cayenne pepper, seasoning* and cooking terms: *boil, poach, garnish.*

Sentence level

Identify and collect instructional verbs, e.g. *boil, poach, cover, shell, chop, add*. Discuss the fact that singular and plural of fish is the same word. Does the same apply to haddock?

Discuss why words such as *butter, water, parsley* do not generally have a plural.

Text level

Discuss the purpose and format of a typical recipe, i.e. a list of ingredients followed by the method.

Group work and individual writing

Find other recipes, including simple ones suitable for use in school. Discuss the terms 'recipe book' and 'cookery book' and look at examples.

Copy out and display simple recipes for favourite foods.

Year 4 activities

Word level

Collect words and phrases showing degree – *nearly cooked, enough water, tender, moderate, hard, hot.*

Build a dictionary of words with definitions of no more than three words, e.g. *boil – heat until 100 °.*

Check spelling of words with double consonants: *haddock, chopped.*

Sentence level

Discuss how and why recipes use the present tense, e.g. 'until they are hard'.

Discuss how the short sentences could be joined using connectives.

Text level

Discuss in detail the format of a recipe, i.e. title, background information, list of ingredients with quantities. Method in chronological order, serving information.

Discuss the use of the imperative in instructional writing.

Group work and individual writing

Rewrite part of the method in the first person, past tense, e.g. 'While I was boiling the rice I put the fish in a frying pan …' Alternatively use first person plural, e.g. 'First we boiled the rice …'

Year 5 activities

Word level

Use a thesaurus to find synonyms for selected words in the passage, e.g. *garnish – decorate, trim, adorn, embellish.*

Use a dictionary to find the range of meanings for words such a *poach, season, tender, round.*

Sentence level

Rewrite some of the abbreviated sentences such as 'Serves four' at greater length.

Identify and discuss words and phrases that denote time, e.g. at the same time, until, then, before.

Text level

Discuss how recipes use abbreviated form, e.g. 'Boil the rice until nearly cooked' rather than 'until it is nearly cooked'. Discuss whether the recipe could be abbreviated further, e.g. in the sentence 'Melt butter in frying pan', what words can be omitted and what key words must be left in?

Group work and individual writing

Discuss how television cookery programmes present recipes in different ways. Script and present (with imaginary ingredients) a television show (perhaps with a flamboyant presenter) showing the audience how to cook kedgeree.

Decide whether a diagram would be helpful for any part of the recipe. How could the recipe be presented visually, for example for people who could not read English?

Year 6 activities

Word level

Discuss qualifying words that could be added to the passage and whether they would be useful or not, e.g. *carefully* shell … *gently* poach the *delicious* fish …

Sentence level

Discuss the use of the colon to introduce a list. Revise the structure and purpose of the recipe.

Text level

Discuss how some parts of the recipe are optional, and how recipes can be a series of rigid instructions or a guide which the individual cook can vary to suit their own taste. Discuss parts of the recipe where judgement is required, e.g. 'until tender'.

Which sorts of instructions need to be adhered to rigidly, and which are just a guide? Discuss ideas such as how to repair a puncture or what to do in a fire, contrasted with cooking recipes, and guides on how to write a poem or design a garden.

In what ways do recipes differ from sets of rules?

Group work and individual writing

Discuss how the recipe formula could be used in other contexts, e.g. in instruction for self-assembly furniture or model kits. Find examples of 'non food recipes'.

Use the recipe formula for more imaginative writing including poetry, e.g. a recipe for a wonderful day, a recipe for a creepy story, a recipe for an alien.

Write a brief description of kedgeree as it might appear on a menu.

Thesaurus, Dictionary, Glossary extracts

Activities for all years

The examples of entries in a thesaurus and dictionary allow the teacher to work with a group to explain their use. The word selected, *rush*, is taken from Non-fiction: Travelling to school.

Thesaurus

Discuss the range of synonyms offered by the thesaurus, and what particular shade of meaning and specific contexts some or each word or phrase has. The word comes from the compound *rush-hour* used in the travelling to school: create new compounds such as *scurry-hour* (a busy time for mice!) and so on.

Dictionary

Talk about the range of meanings for the word *rush*, and how each meaning can have a set of words depending on the part of speech – *rushy, rushlike*. Discuss how some meanings are only used in a specific, technical context (the first print of a film) and how other meanings have become obsolete (the cattle disease). Use a more extensive dictionary to find further compound words, e.g. gold-rush, and the origins of some of the other definitions.

Glossary

Use these pages to demonstrate the use of a glossary. The glossary could be extended by the children to make their own personal word lists.